Halloween was always my favorite time of the year.
The cold windy weather, the color of the leaves changing and
that overall spooky vibe in the air that you feel between
the months of September and November.

The best part is not only can you dress up as your favorite
character or hero but you get a sack full of candy on top of
it. Not to mention the Halloween parties!

I would like to dedicate this book to my two babies.
May they also enjoy the magic that this time of the year brings.

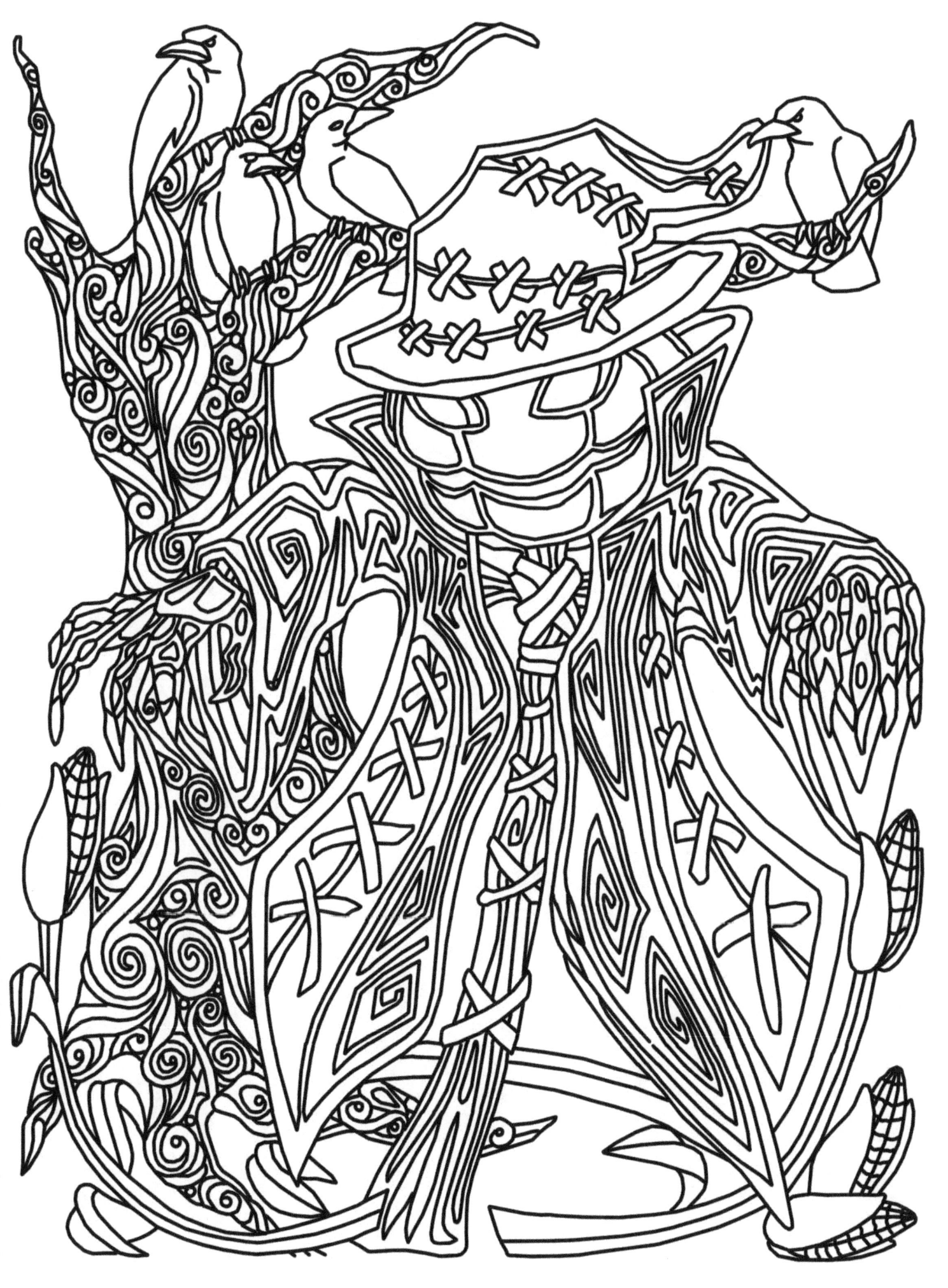

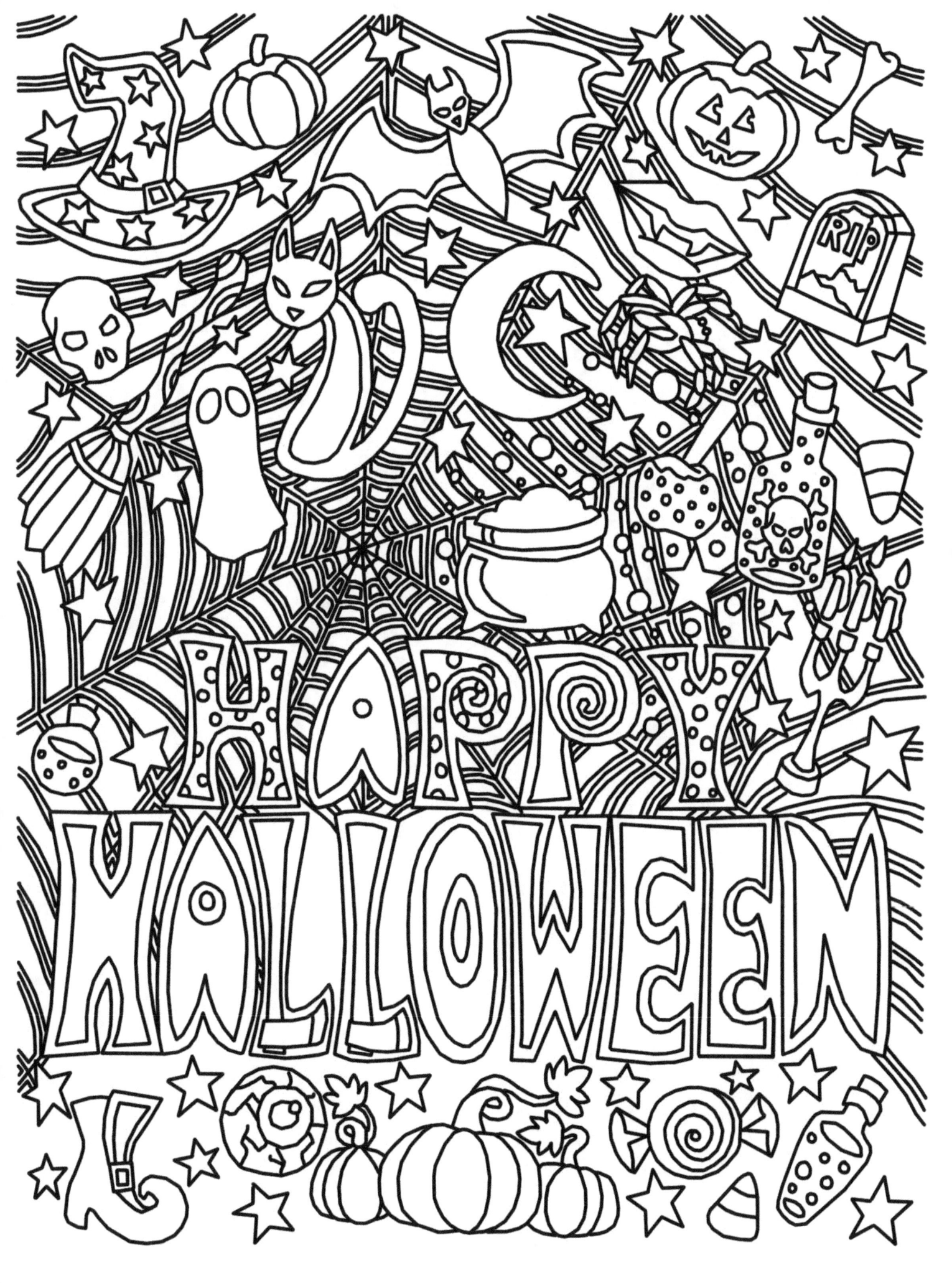

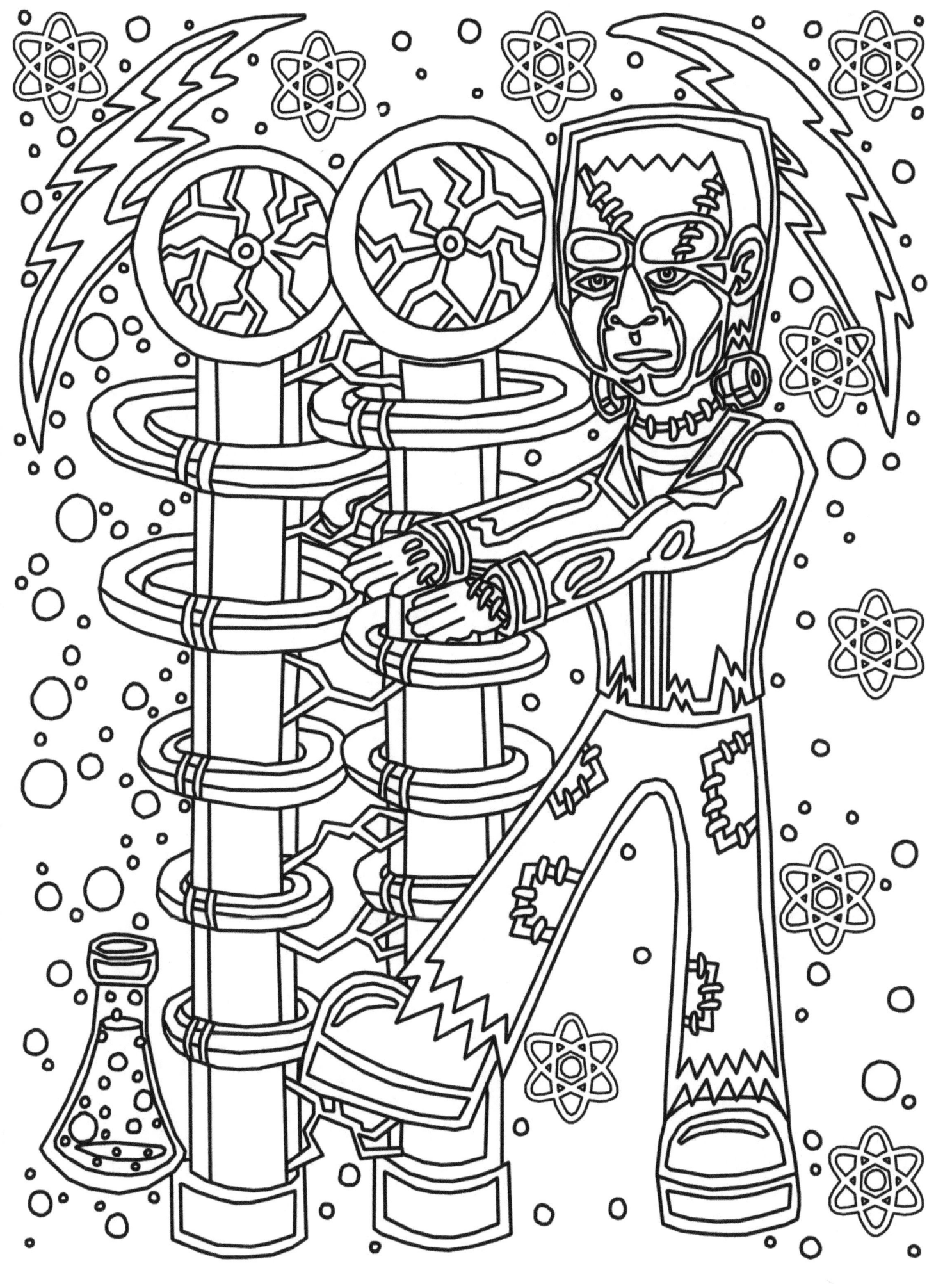

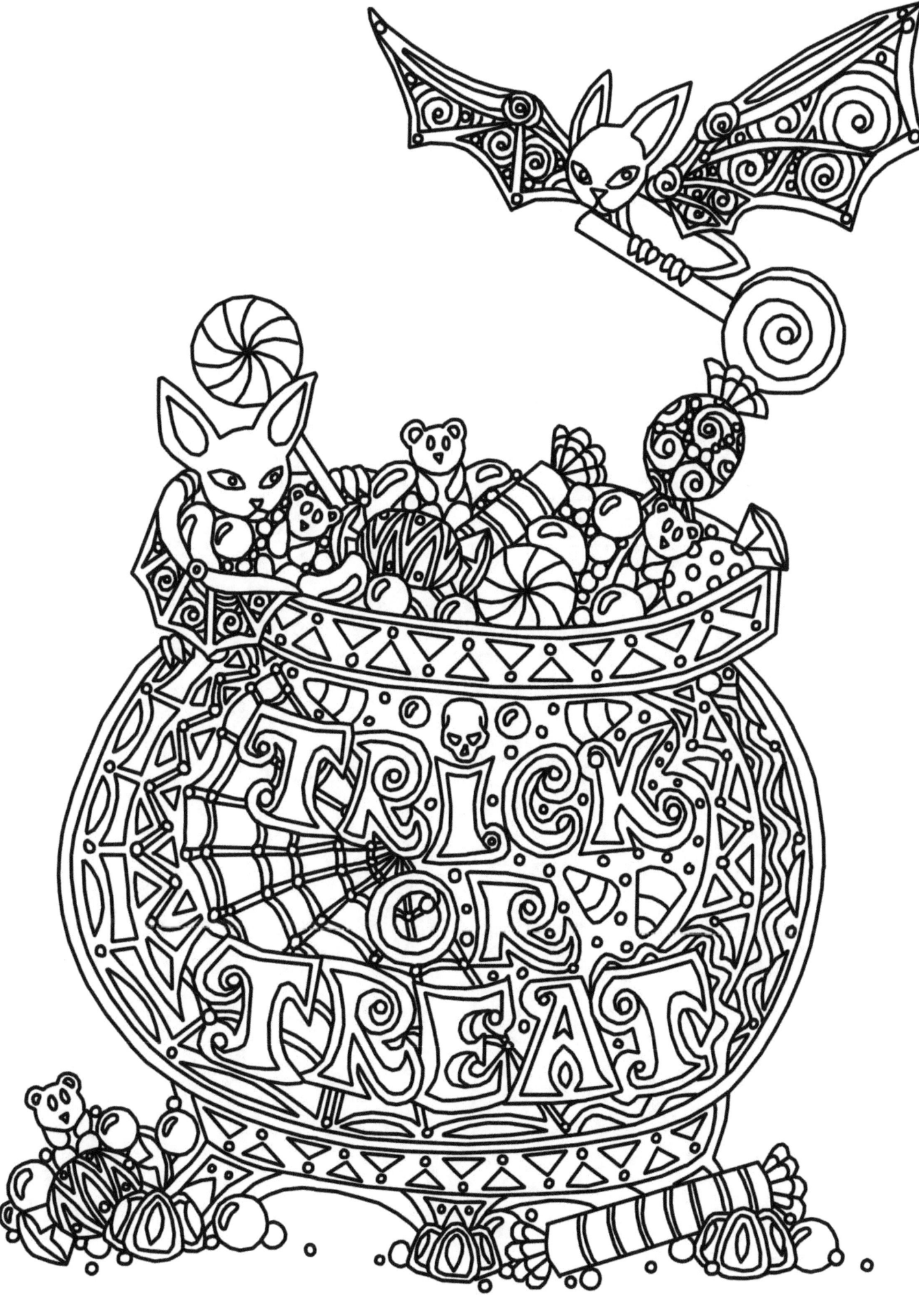

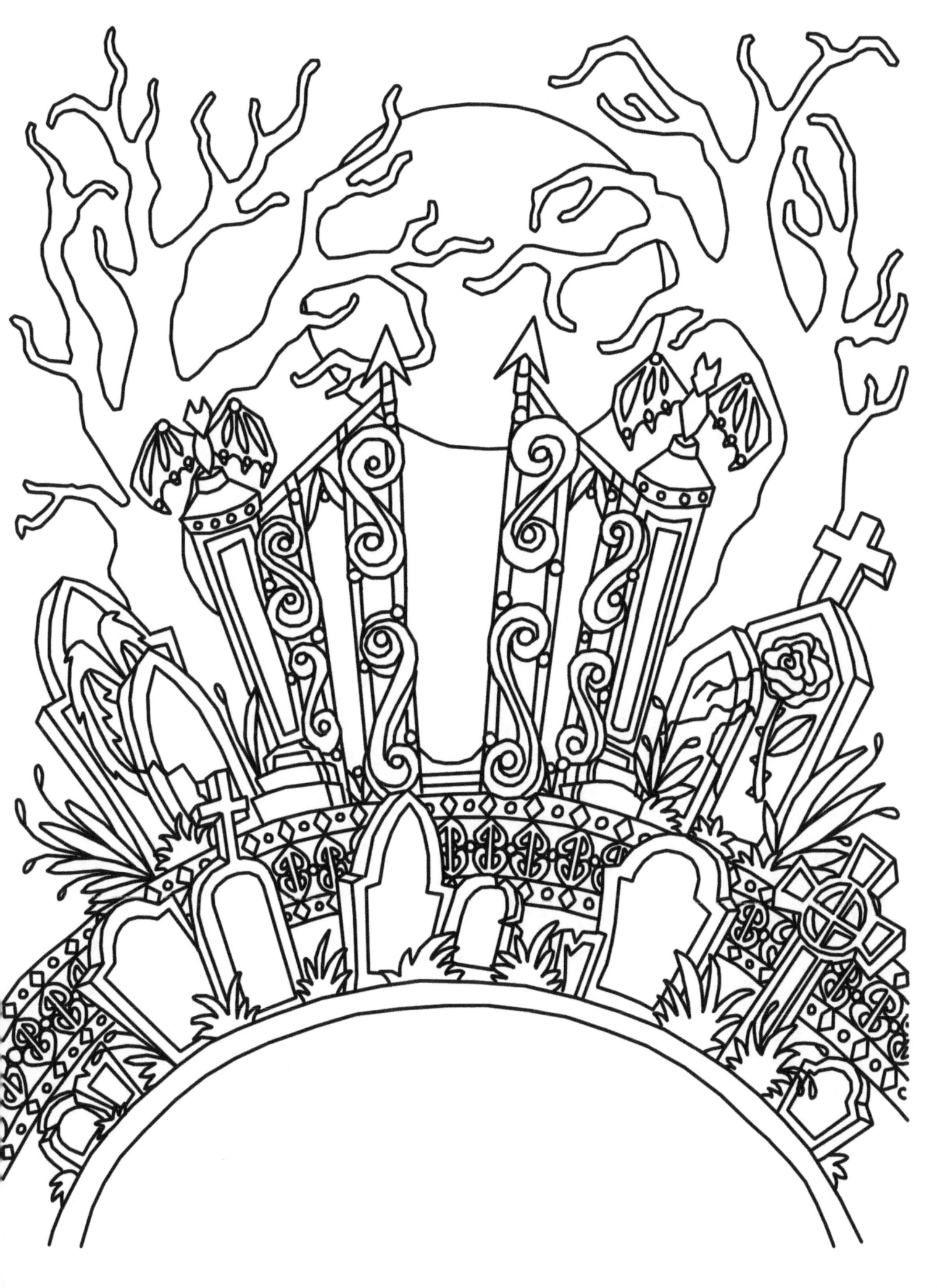

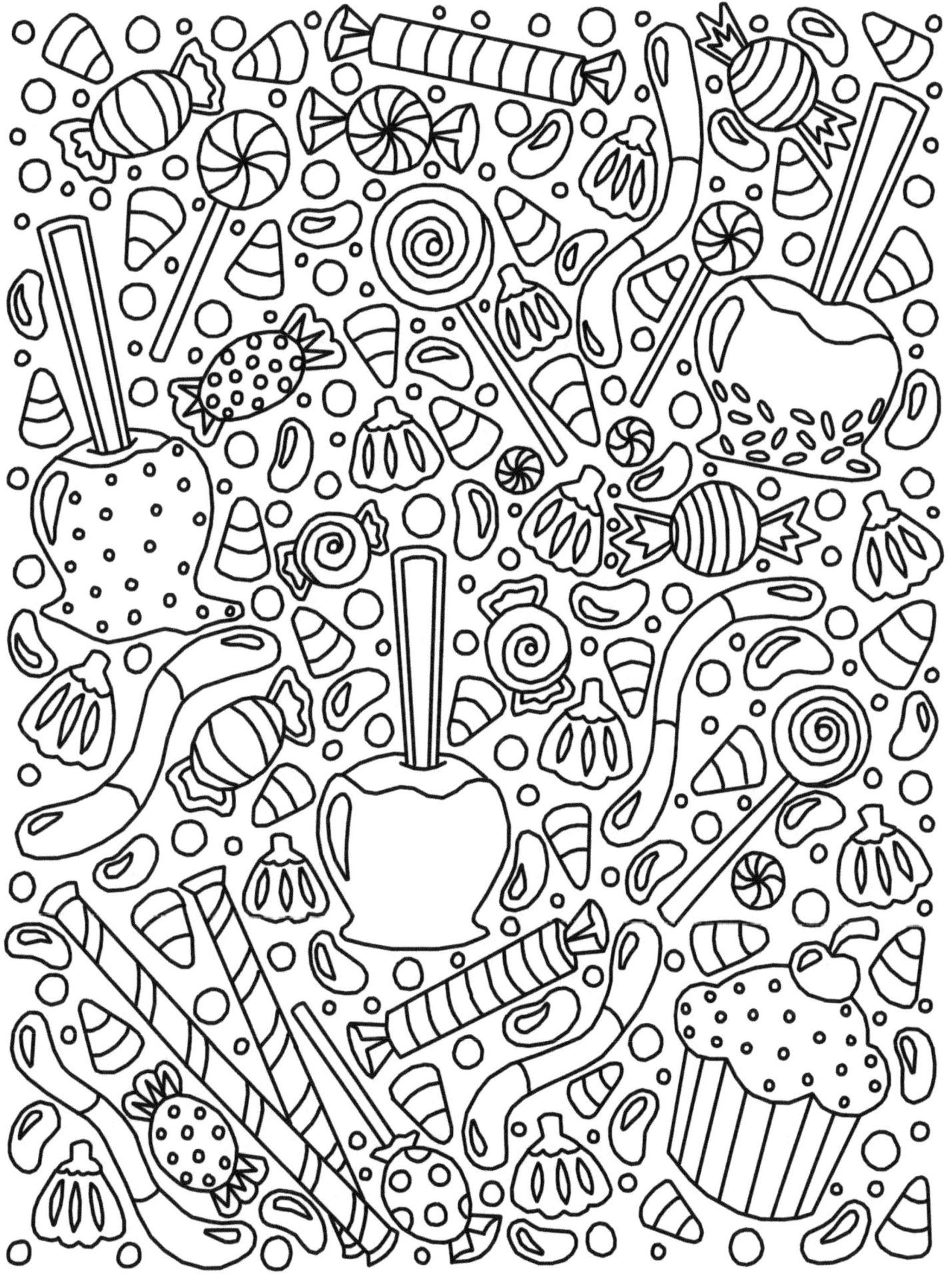

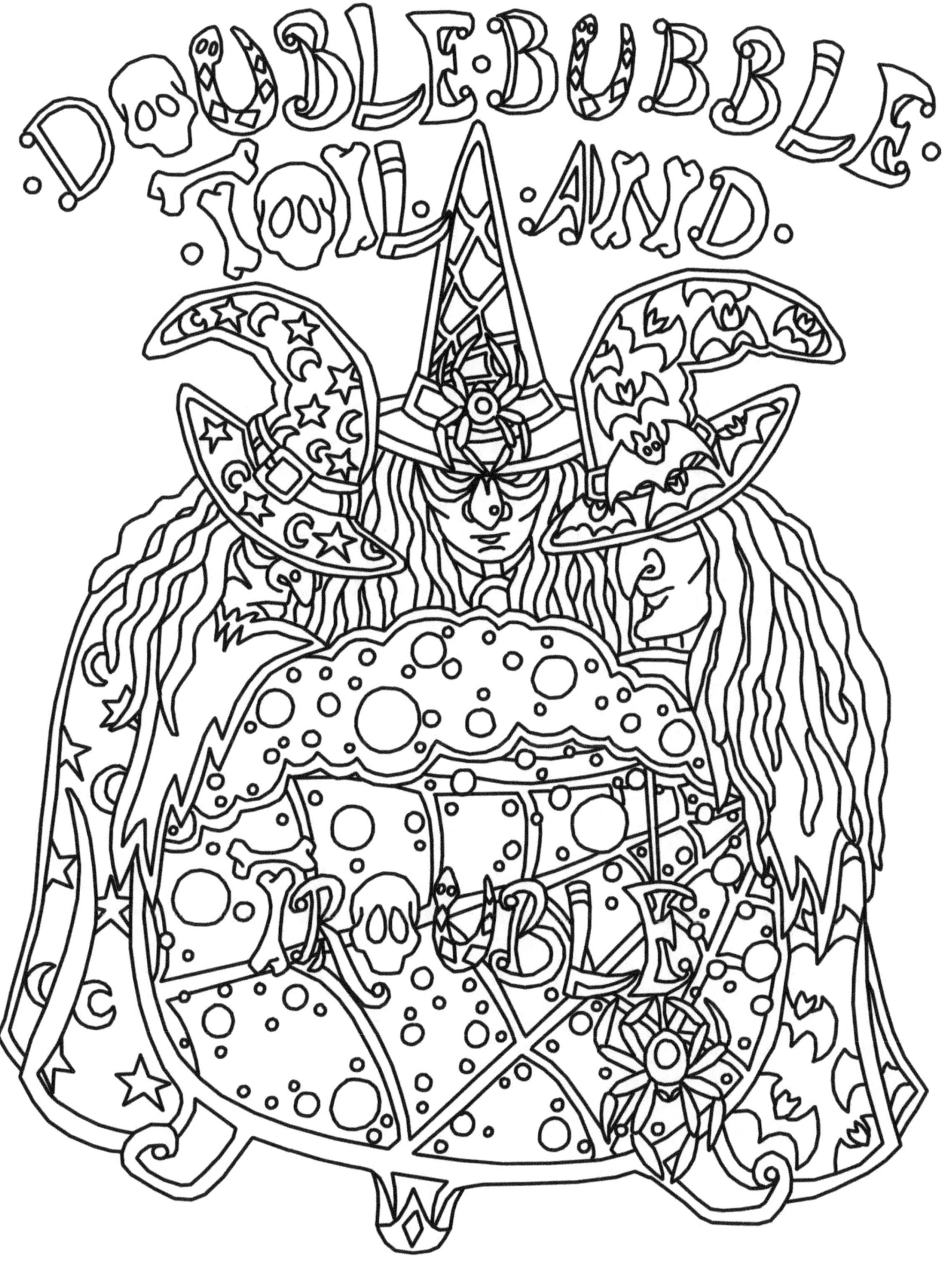

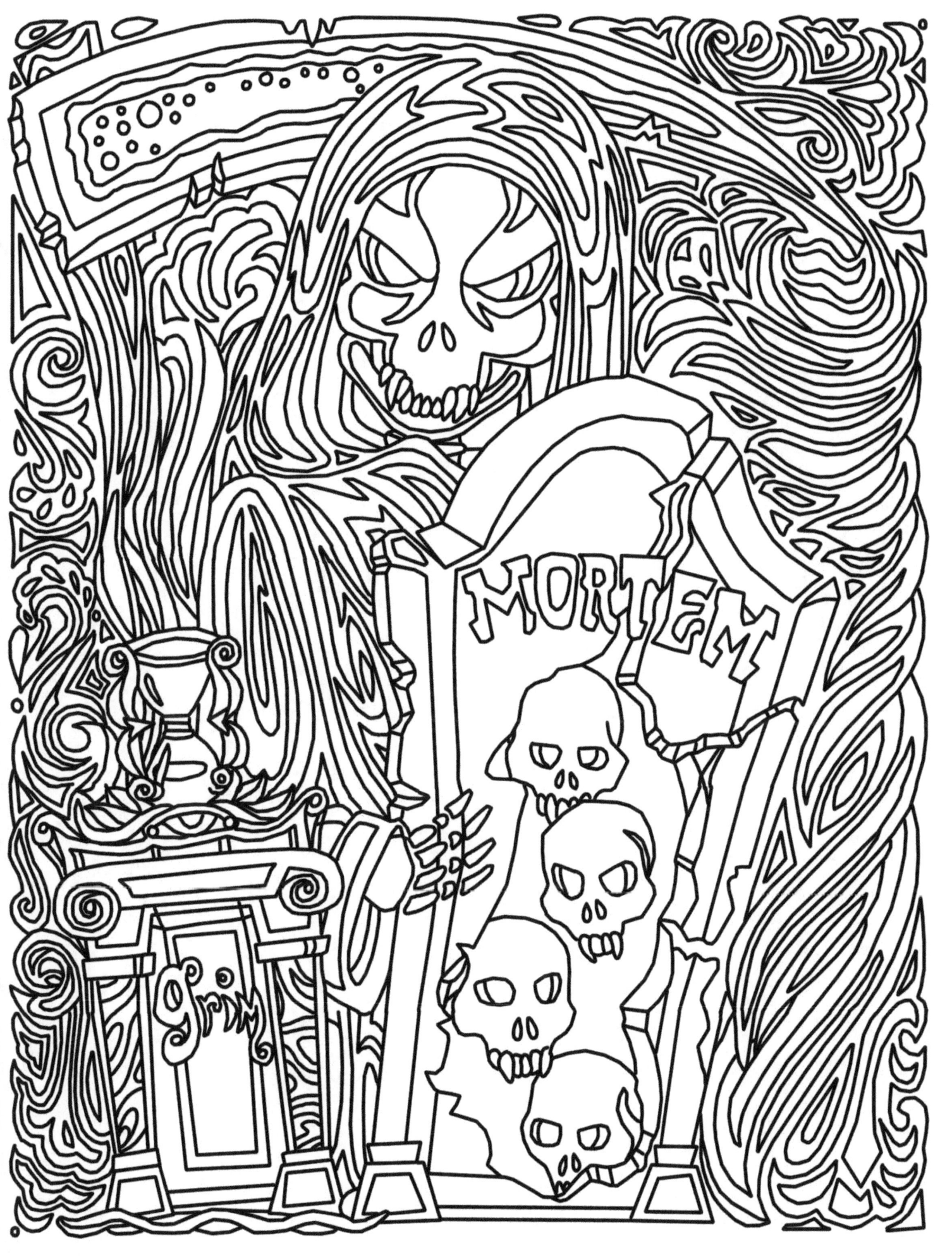

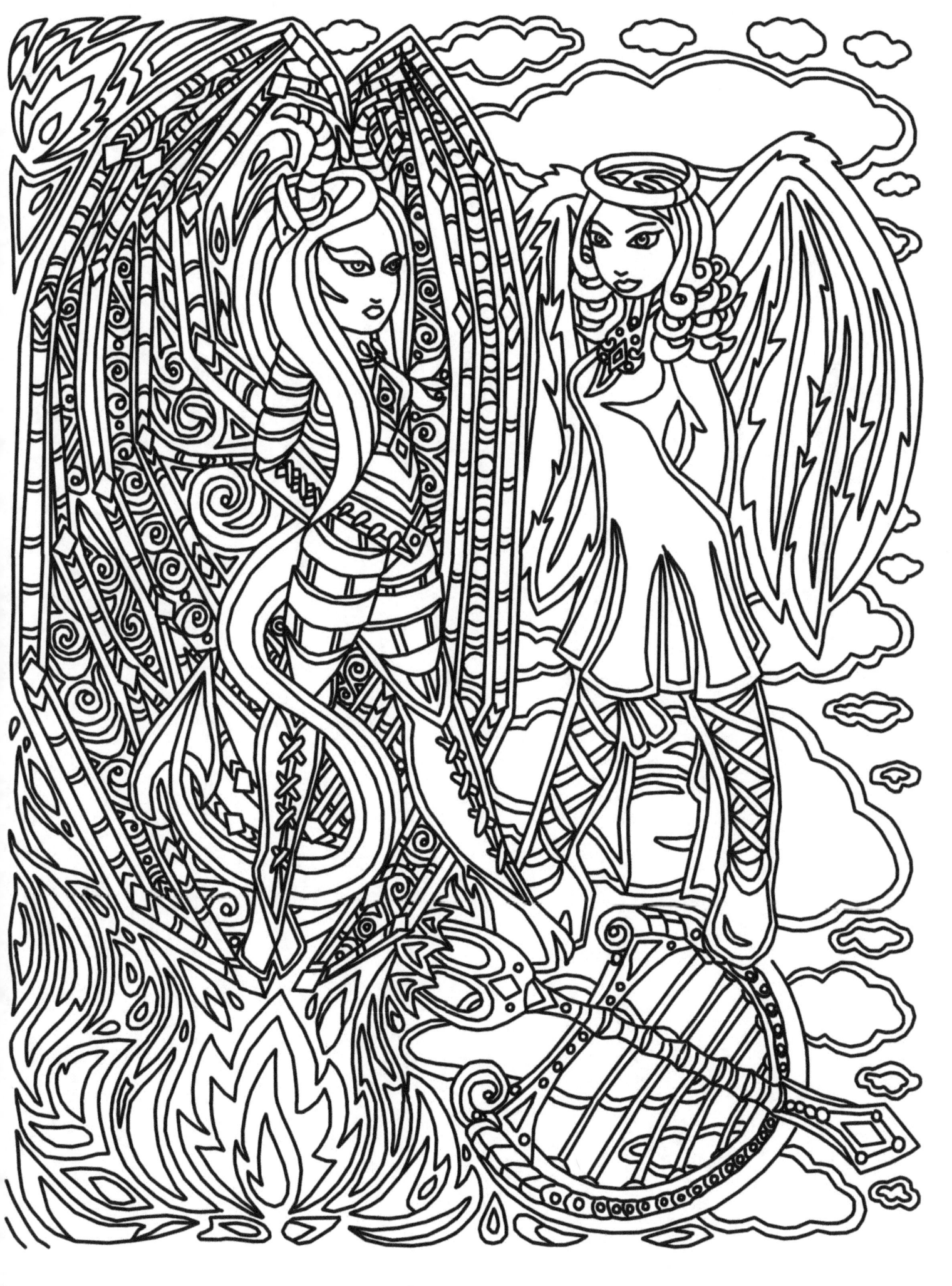

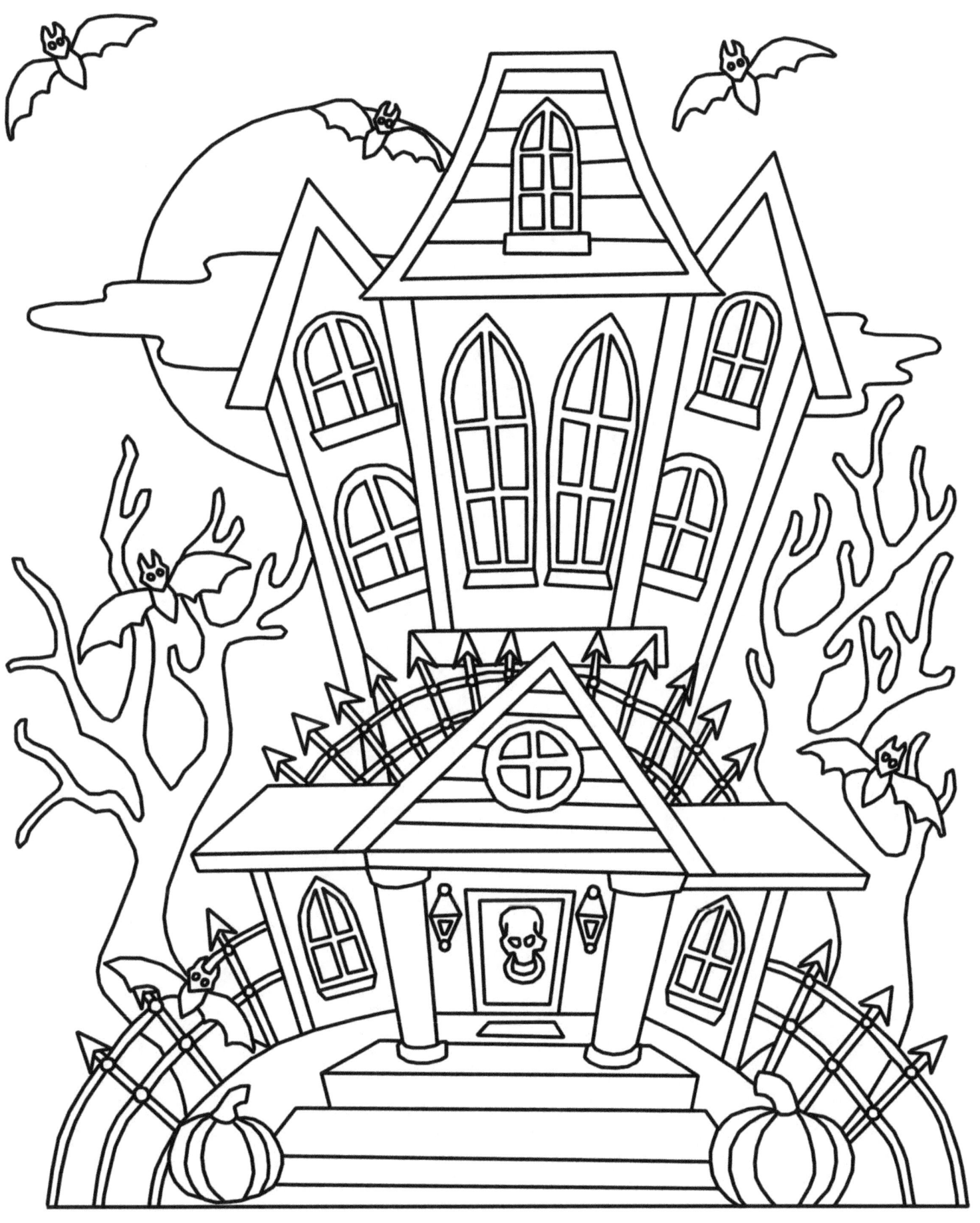

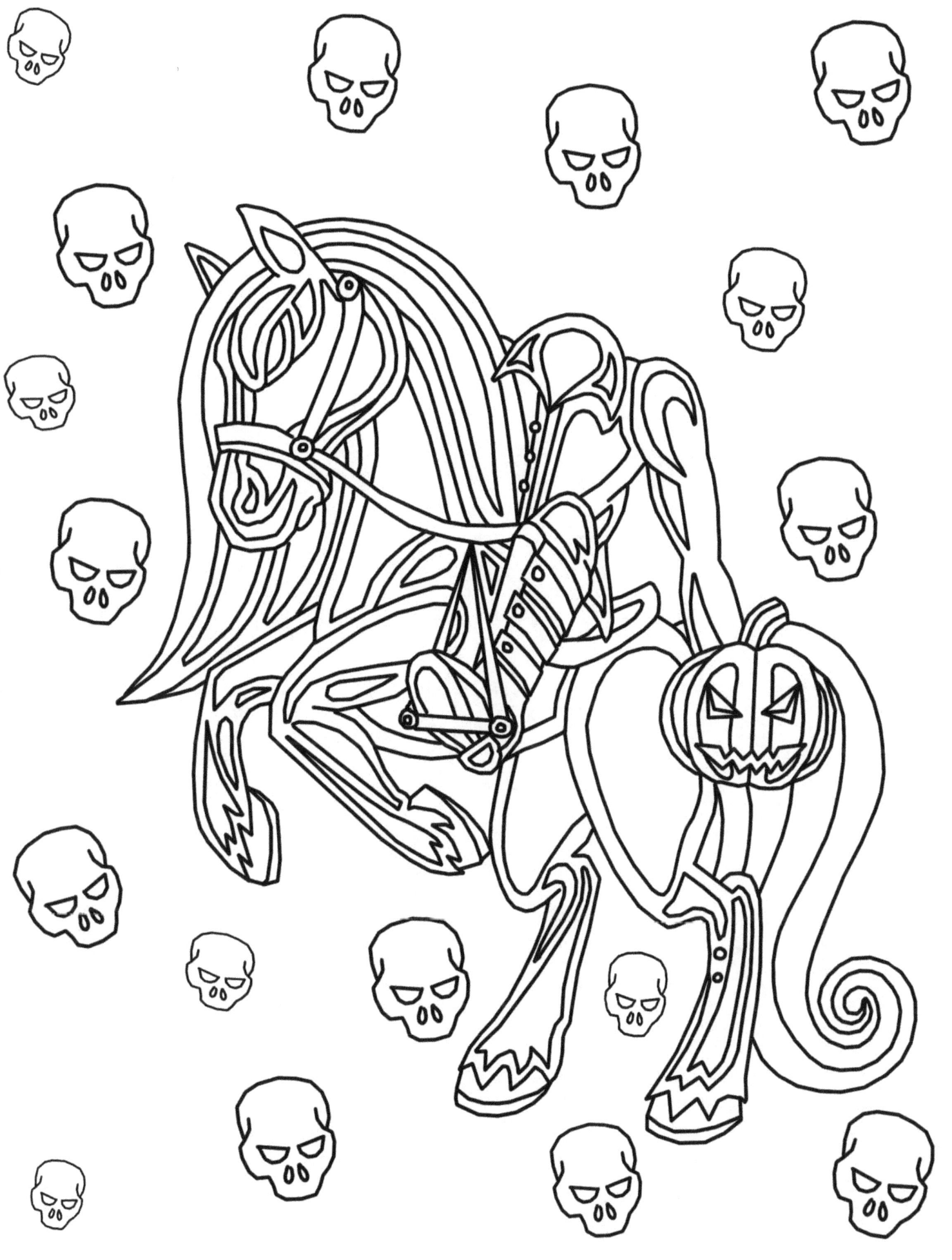

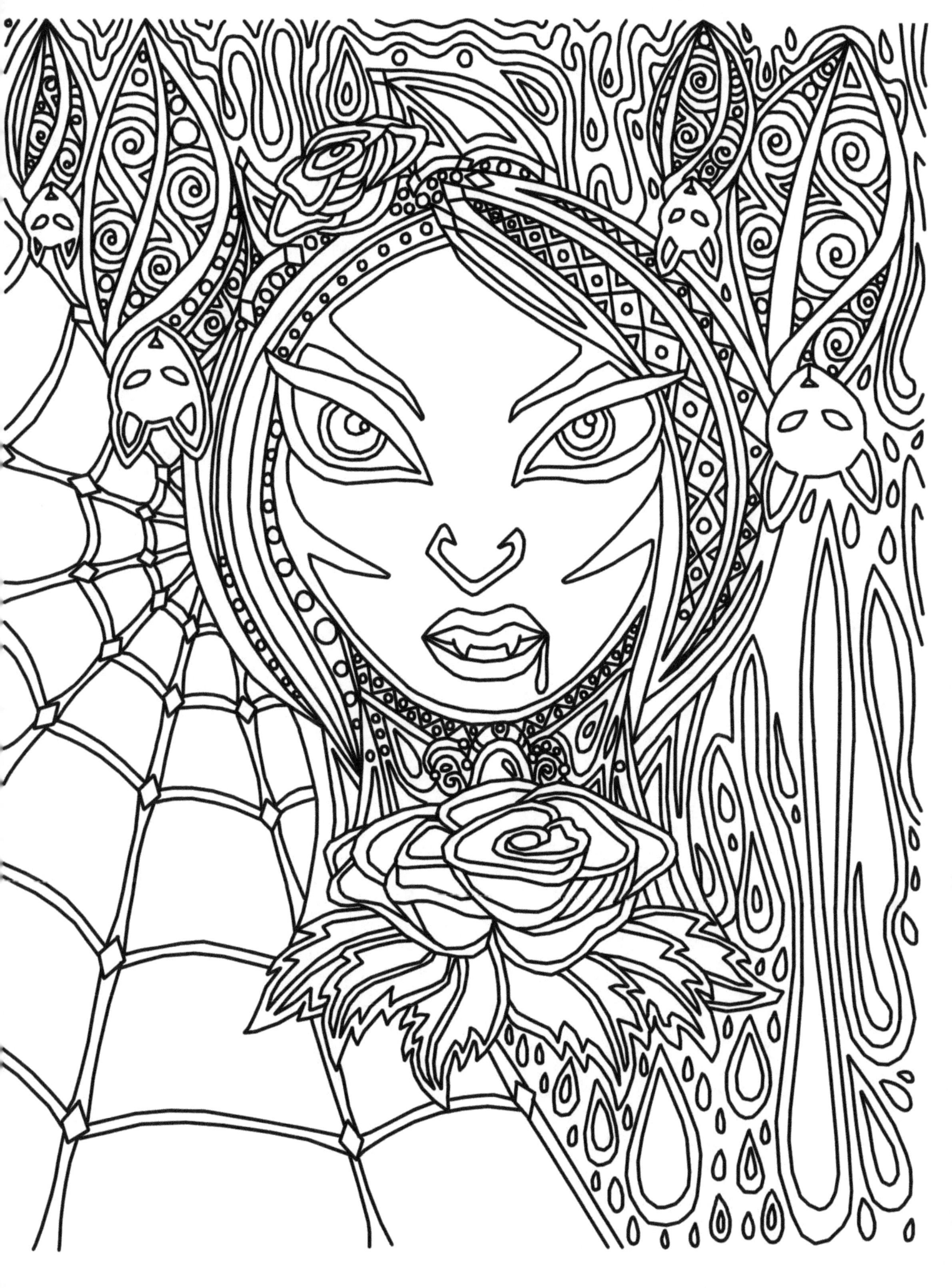

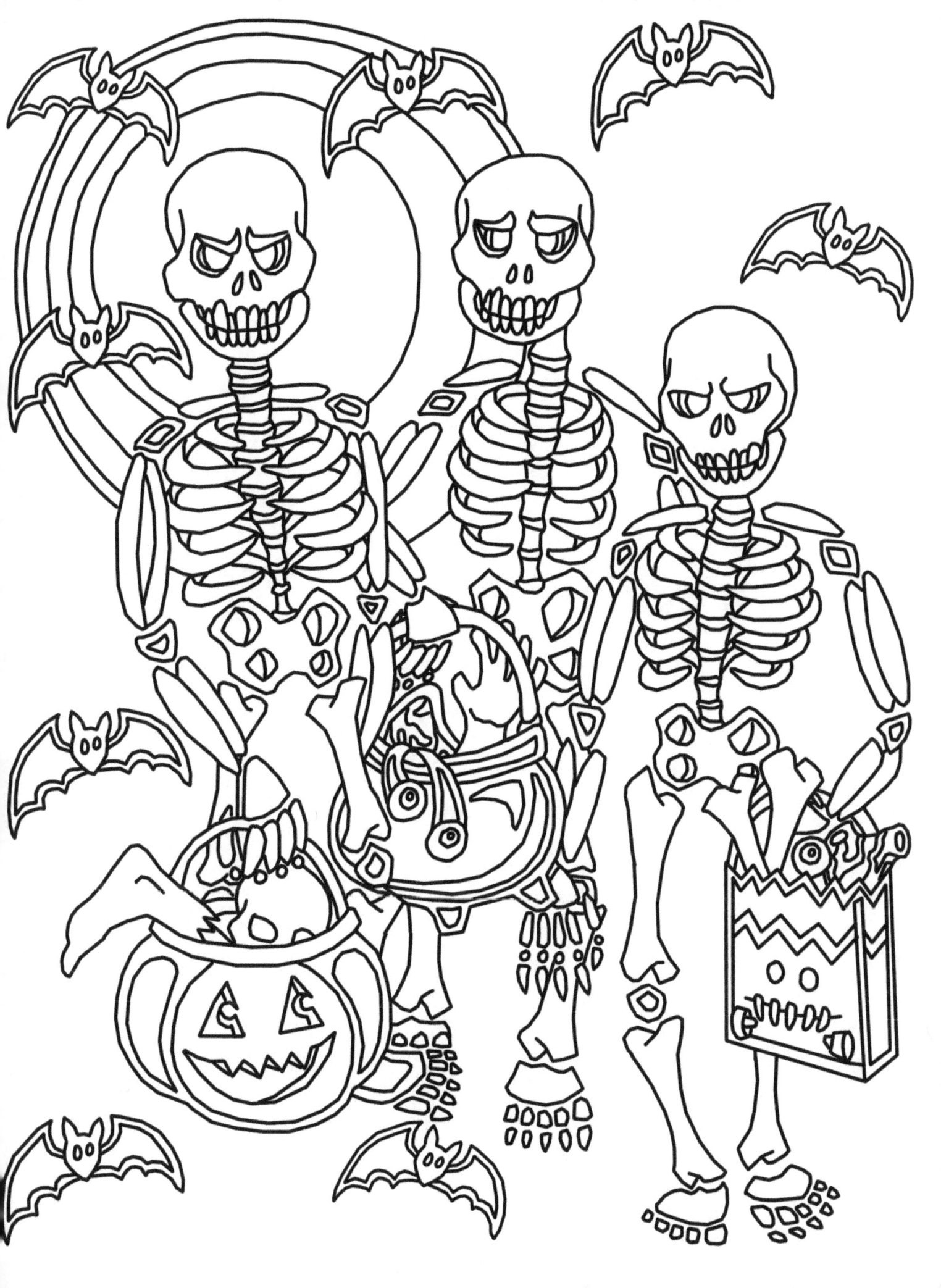

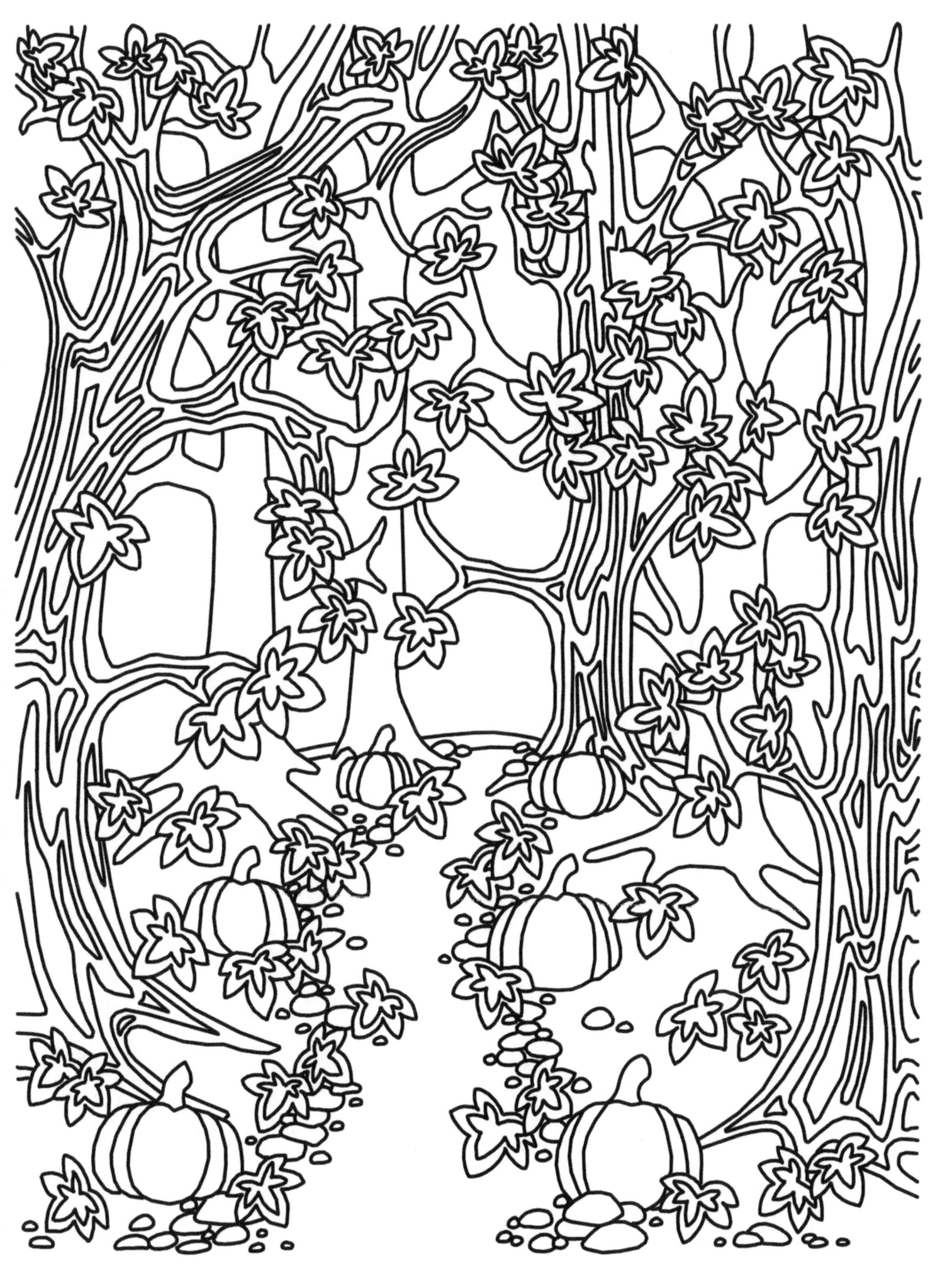

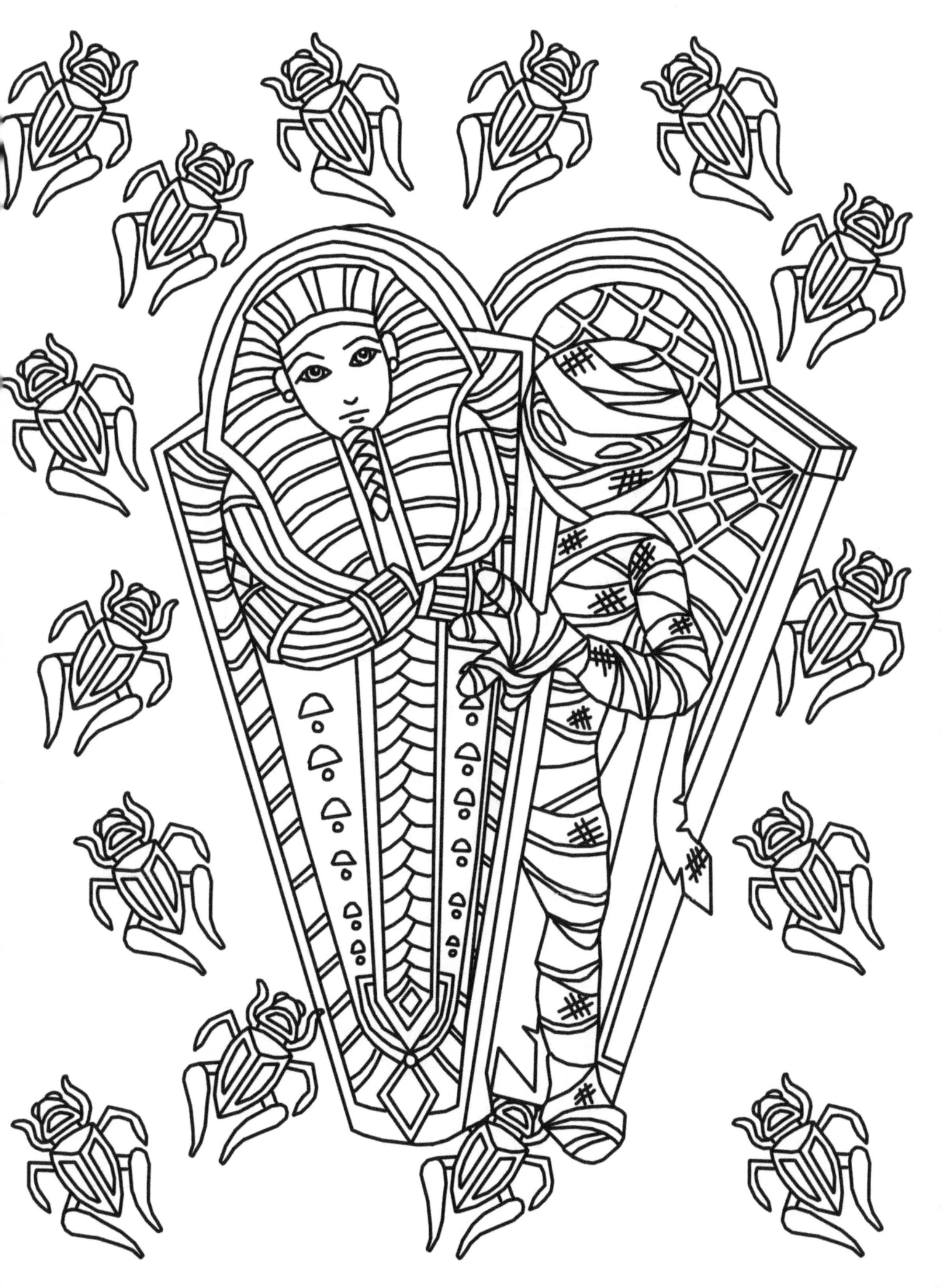

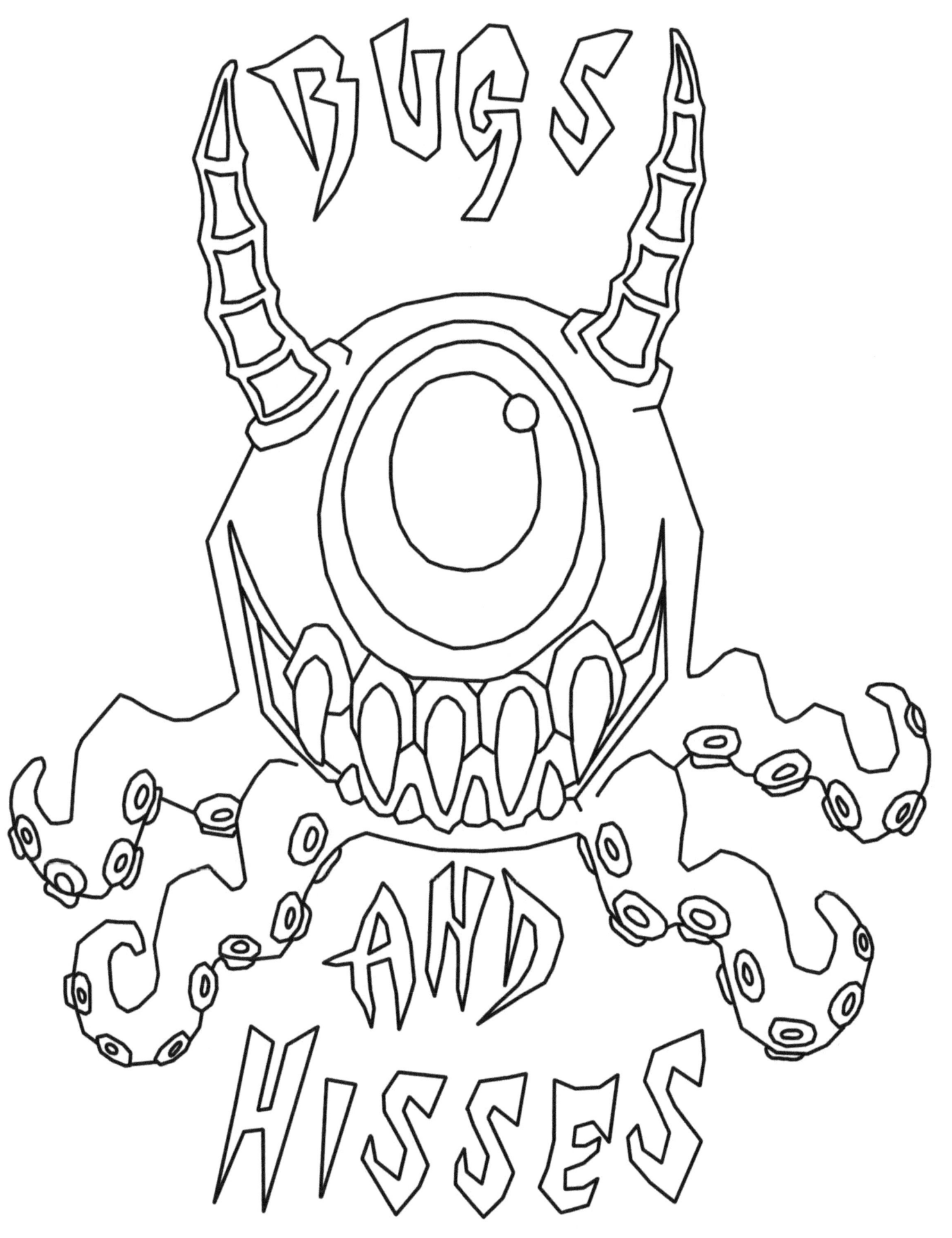

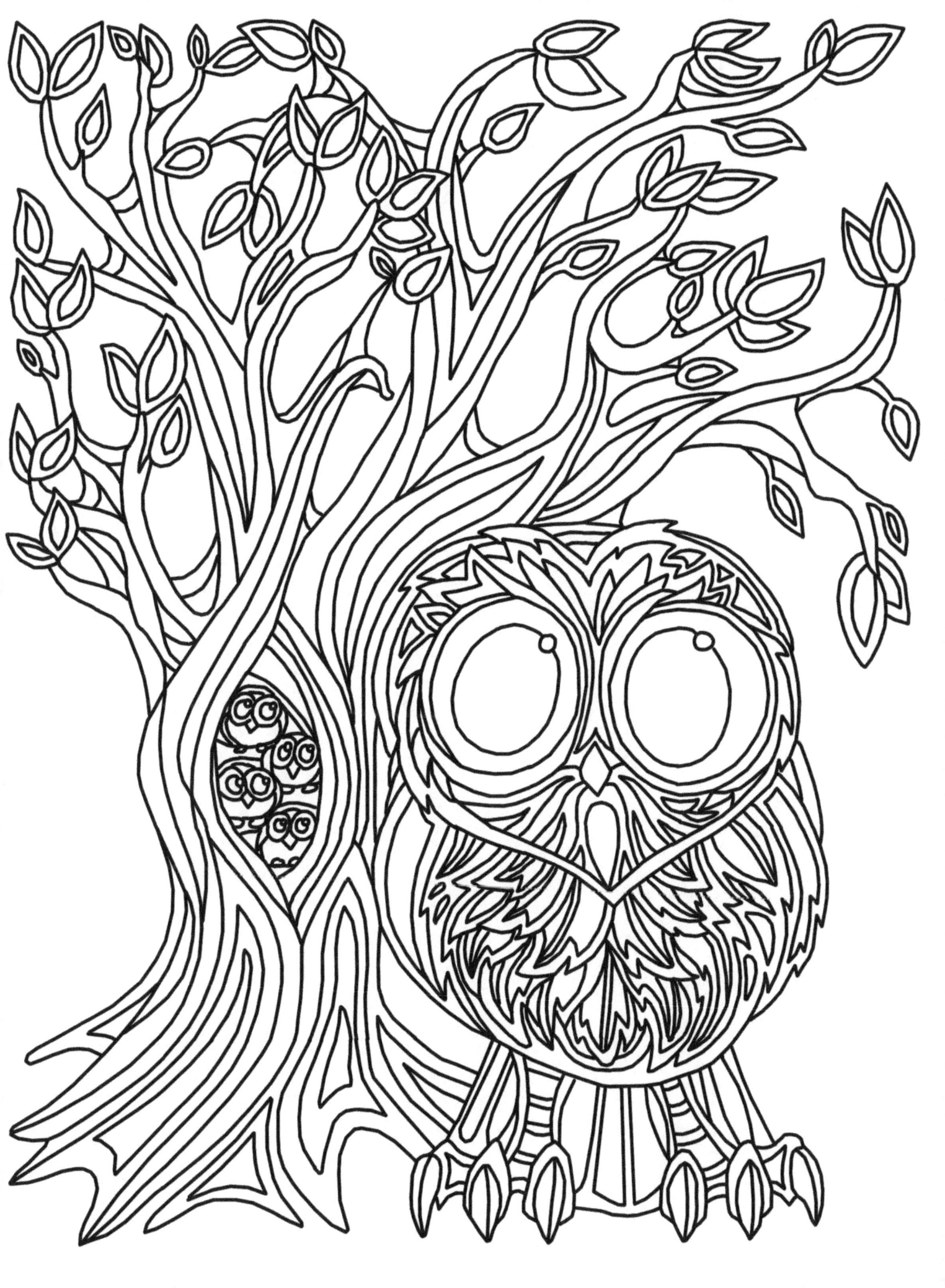

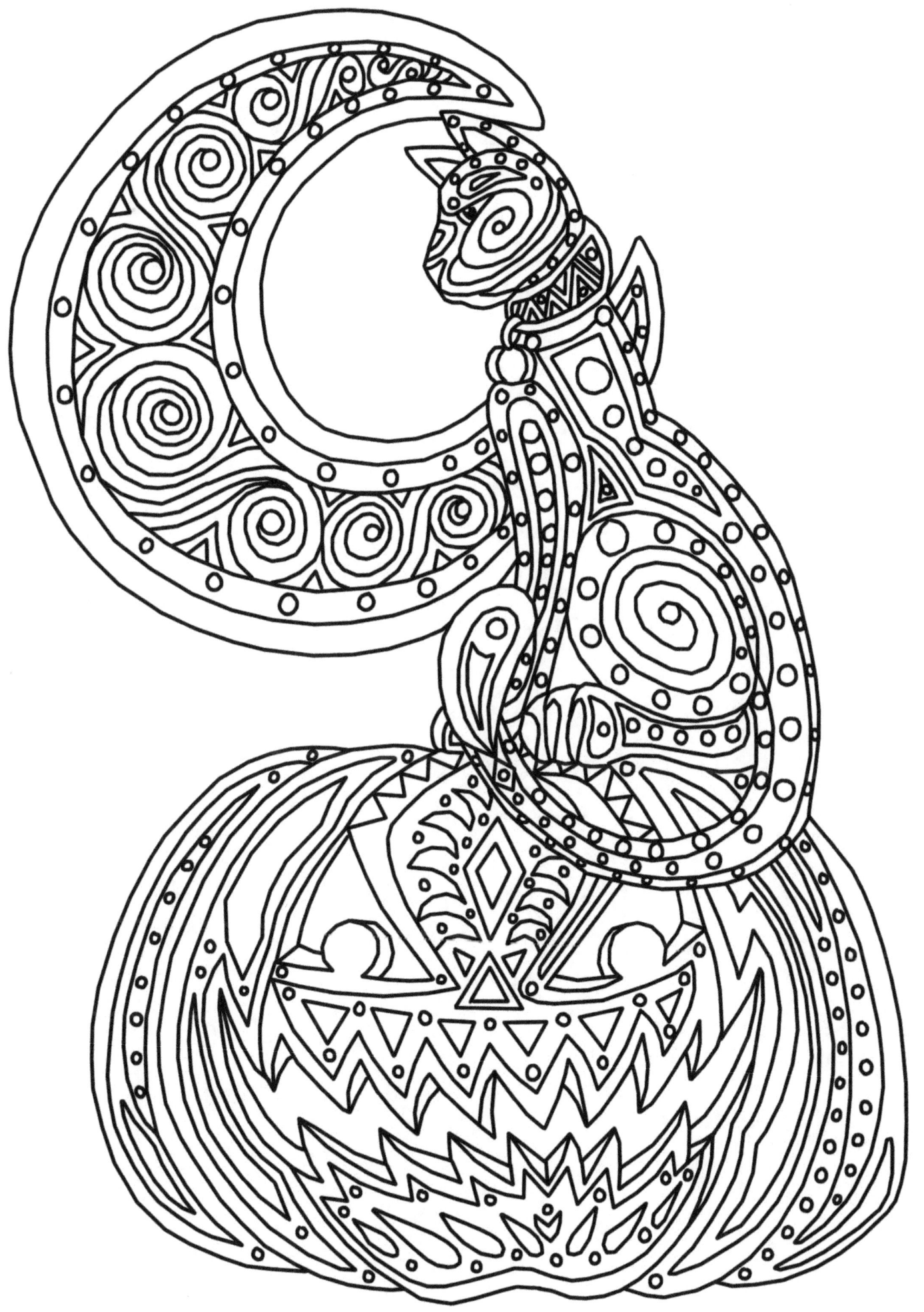

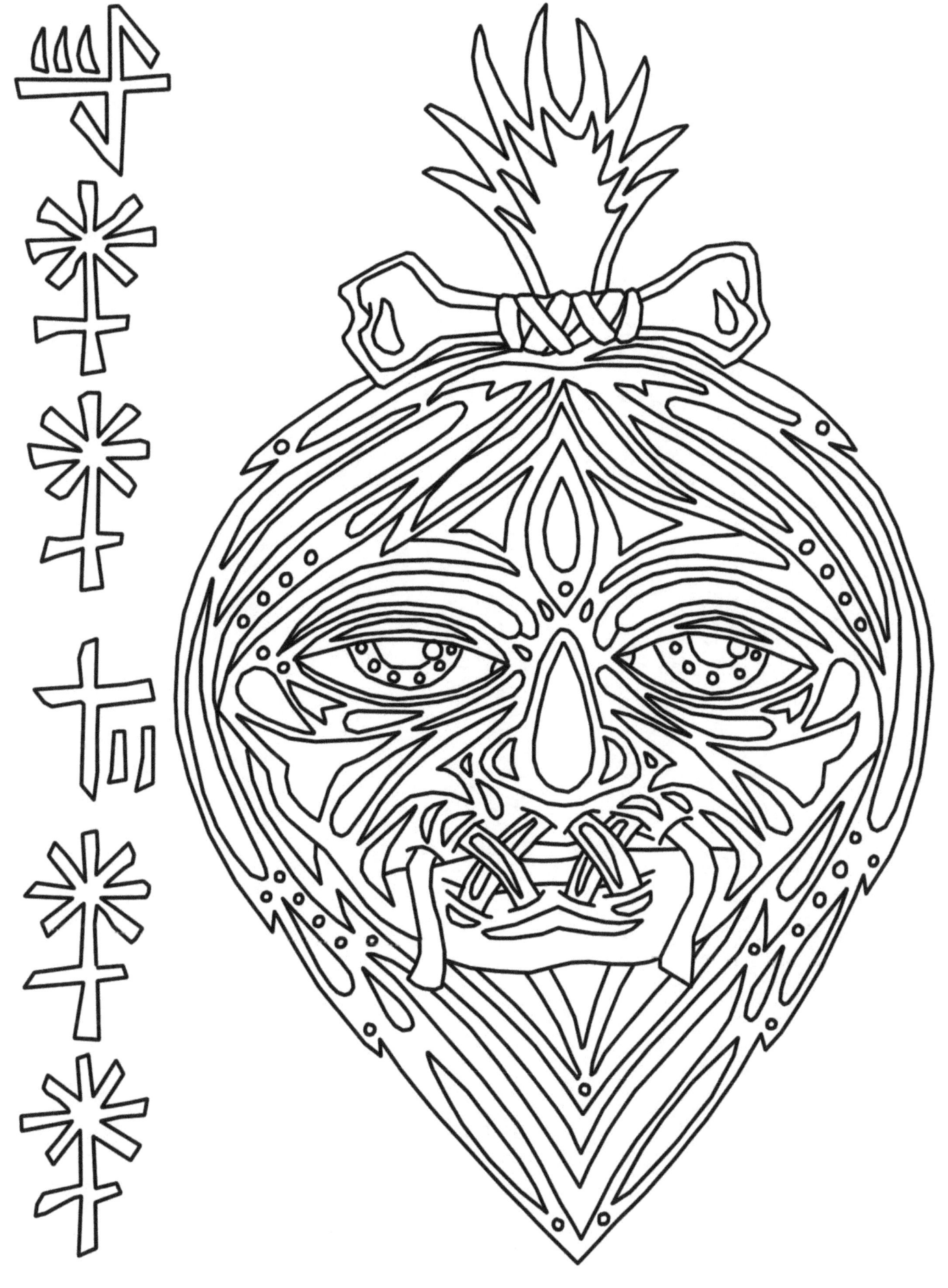

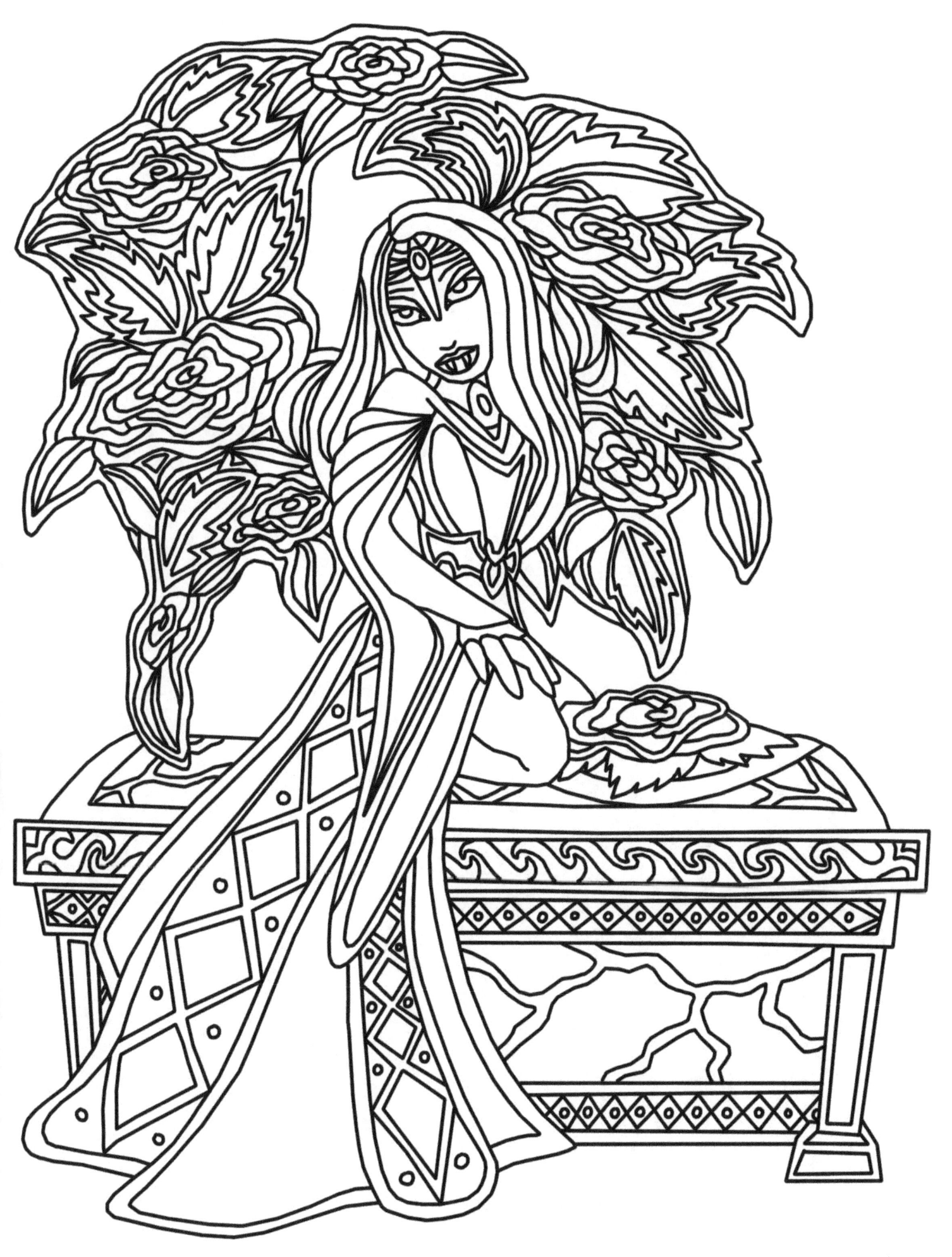

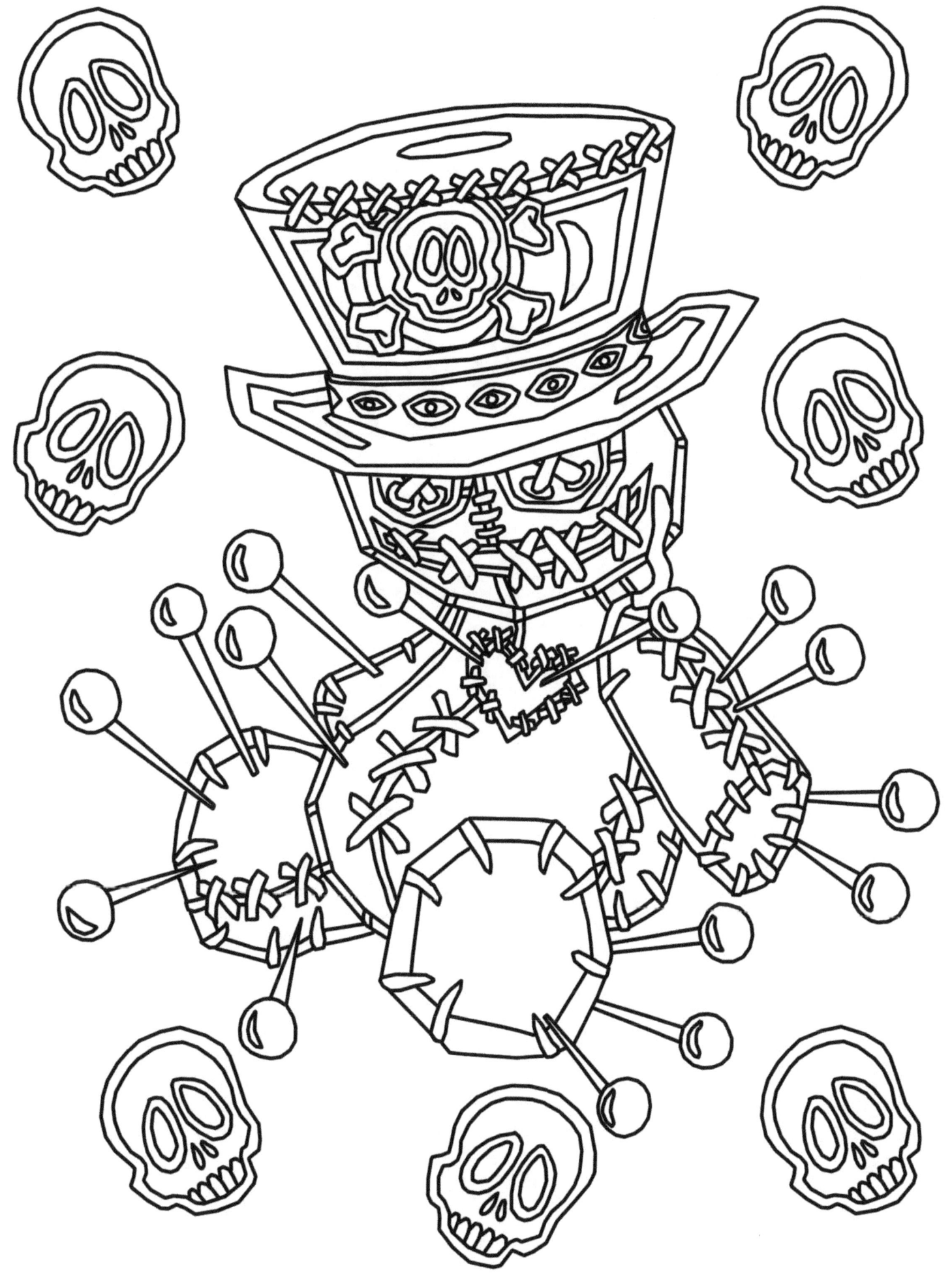

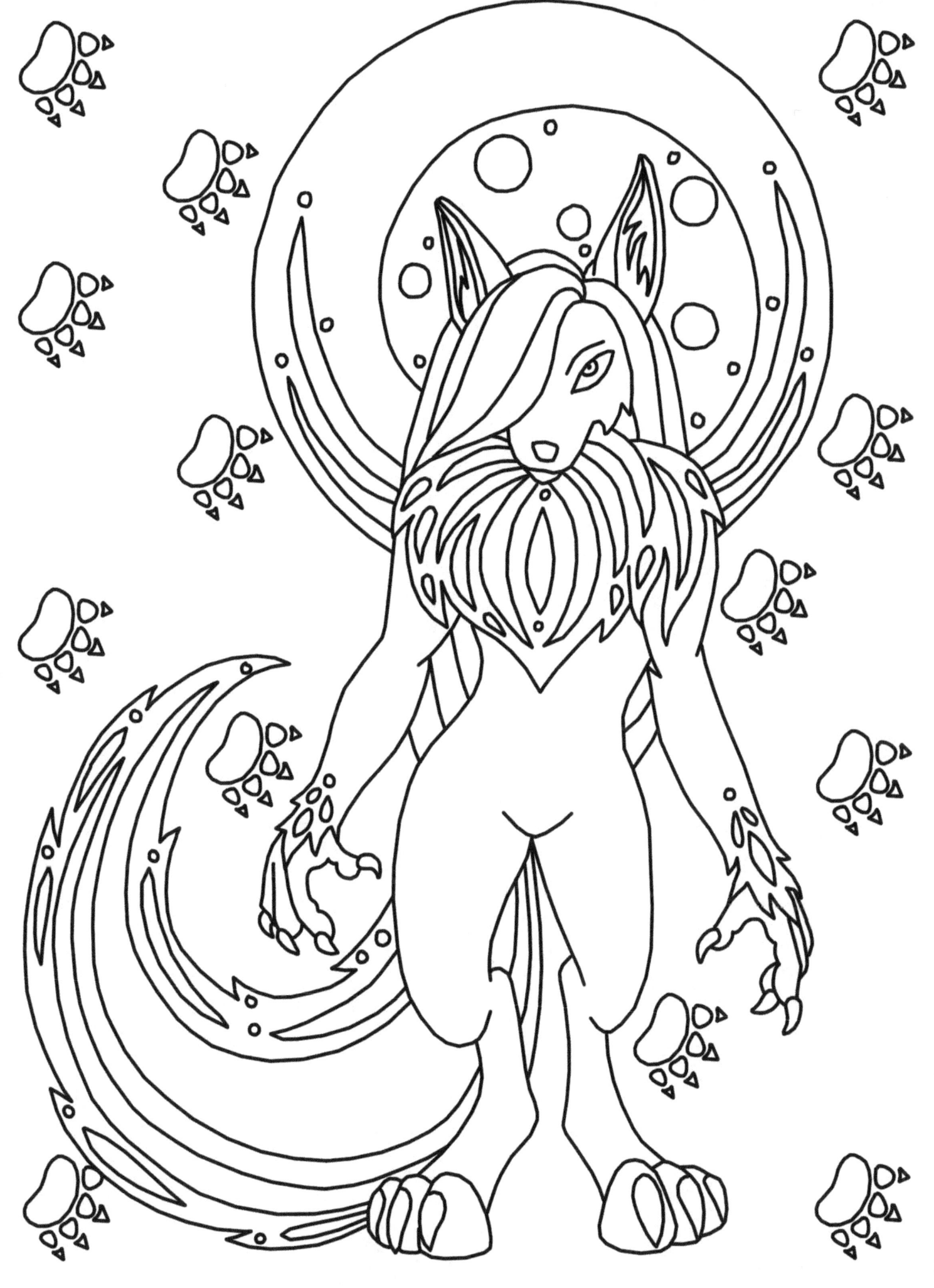

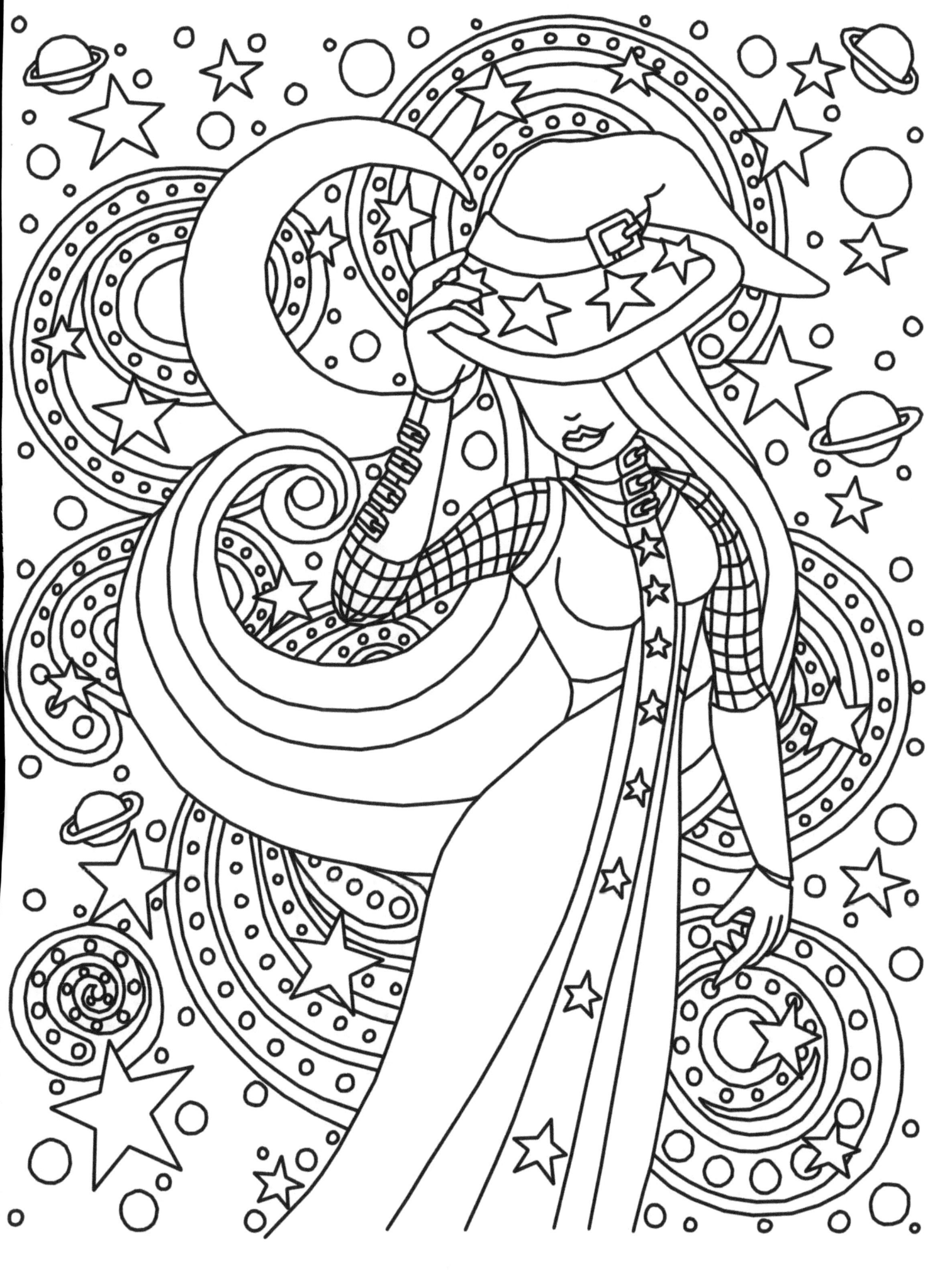

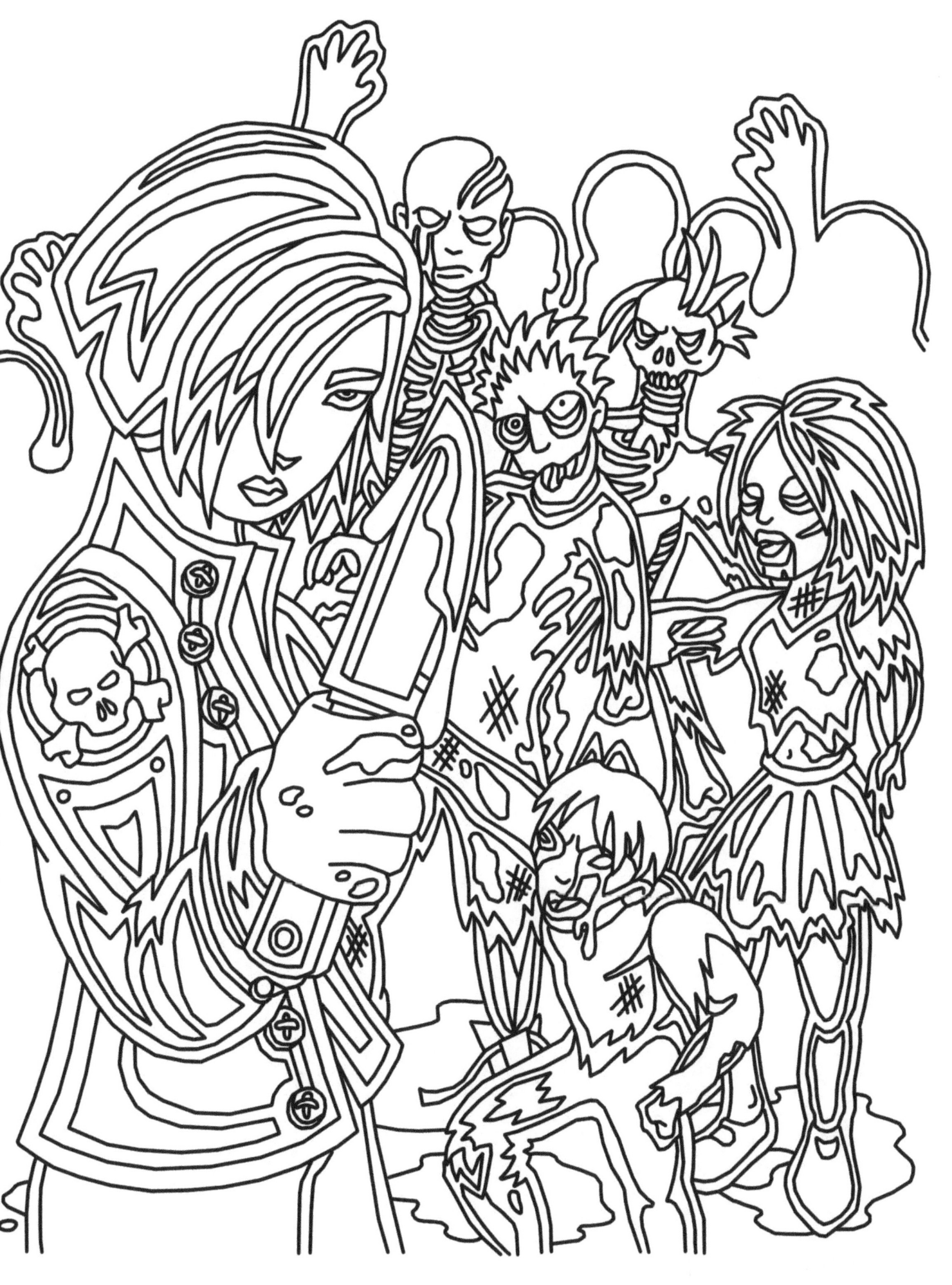